HIS MANNERS & CHARACTERISTICS

In the name of Allah the Most Beneficent, Most Merciful

ⓗ المكتب التعاوني للدعوة والإرشاد و توعية الجاليات بالربوة، ١٤٣٨هـ
فهرسة مكتبة الملك فهد الوطنية أثناء النشر

مركز أصول العالمي
سلسلة كتيبات التعريف بالنبي محمد رسول الله - اللغة الإنجليزية. /
مركز أصول العالمي. - الرياض، ١٤٣٩هـ
٤٠ ص، ١١٫٥ سم ١٥ x ١٥ سم
ردمك : ٣-٠٩-٨٢٤٩-٦٠٣-٩٧٨ (مجموعة)
٣-١٢-٨٢٤٩-٦٠٣-٩٧٨ (ج٣)

١- السيرة النبوية   أ. العنوان
ديوي ٢٣٩   ١٤٣٩/٨٤٤

رقم الإيداع: ١٤٣٩/٨٤٤
ردمك : ٣-٠٩-٨٢٤٩-٦٠٣-٩٧٨ (مجموعة)
٣-١٢-٨٢٤٩-٦٠٣-٩٧٨ (ج٣)

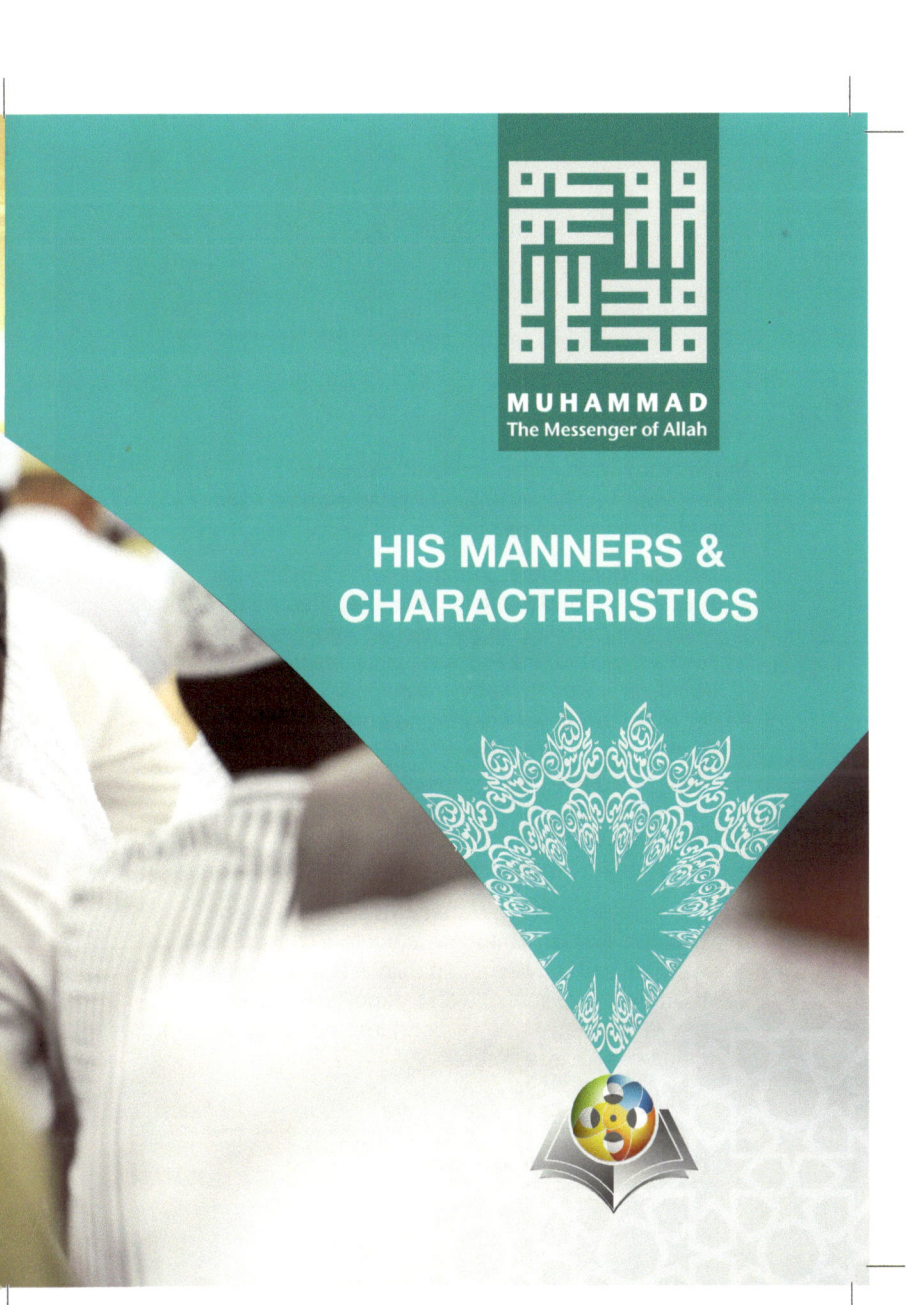

Terms

Terminology used in this series of booklets.
(Taken from Sheikh Mahmoud Murad's book, *Common Mistakes in Translation*).

Rubb: Some prefer to translate the term "Rubb" into "Lord". Beside the fact that the latter is a Biblical term referring to the alleged lordship of the servant of God, the Prophet Jesus, the word lord, which is limited to mean: master, chief, proprietor, or ruler, can never convey the conclusive significance of the term "Rubb". Among other meanings, the term "Rubb" means: the Creator, the Fashioner, the Provider, the One upon Whom all creatures depend for their means of subsistence, and the One Who gives life and causes death.

Deen: The word translated as religion is "Deen", which in Arabic commonly refers to a way of life, which is both private and public. It is an inclusive term meaning: acts of worship, political practice, and a detailed code of conduct, including hygiene or etiquette matters.

Sal'lal'laahu a'laihi wa sal'lam **:** This Arabic term means, "may God praise him and render him safe from all evil."

BOOKLET 3

This booklet is the third in a series of publications based on a book titled *Muhammad, the Messenger of Allah*. Each booklet covers an aspect of the Prophet's life, deeds and teachings, and aims to provide a better understanding of Muhammad's life and Islamic values.

INTRODUCTION

All praise is due to Allah, the Rubb of the worlds, and may Allah exalt the mention of His Prophet, and render him and his household safe and secure from all derogatory things.

This booklet sheds light on the character of the Prophet Muhammad , and describes him as the greatest individual in history owing directly to his noble manners and his sincere concern for the welfare of his people.

You will also learn how Muhammad lived a normal life though great riches came to him when he became master of this vast Peninsula. He was a great and inspiring leader who led small numbers of people into battles against thousands, and yet he would decisively defeat them. Despite his military strength, he always preferred to resort to peace.

This booklet shares the words of the people who lived at the time

Muhammad used to stand in prayer for so long that his feet would swell. When asked why he did so, he replied, "Should I not then be a thankful slave?"

of the Prophet ﷺ and saw him face-to-face, and who could thus describe him in the greatest detail; his manners, his appearance and his life. The people who saw Muhammad ﷺ described his behavior, how he spoke, how he walked, how he ate, how he treated his family, how he treated his companions, and how he treated his neighbors, among other comprehensive details. Indeed, most of his contemporaries agreed that he was intelligent, sincere, polite, ethical and gentle. Even his enemies admitted that he gave his attention entirely to Islam and how to share Islam with the world.

In all, this booklet mentions thirty six character traits of the Messenger of Allah ﷺ. All of them show that he was the greatest individual in history, and that this is not a baseless claim, for anyone who reads about the Prophet's biography ﷺ and learns of his manners and ethics, keeping aside all preconceived notions, he would certainly reach this exact conclusion.

3

Some of the Prophet's Manners & Characteristics

1 Sound Intellect:

The Messenger ﷺ had an excellent, complete and sound intellect. Qadhi Iyaadh[(1)], may God have mercy on him, said:

"His strong intellect becomes clear when you read his biography and understand his state of affairs, his meaningful and inclusive statements, his good manners, ethics and moral character, his knowledge of the Torah and Gospel and other Divine Scriptures, his knowledge of statements of the wise, his knowledge of bygone nations, his

ability to coin examples, his wisdom in implementing policies and his skill in correcting manners. He was an example and paradigm to which his people could relate to in so many branches of knowledge, acts of worship, medicine, laws of inheritance, lineage, and other matters as well. He knew and learned all of this without reading or examining the Scriptures of those before us, nor did he sit with their scholars. The Prophet had no formal schooling, could not read or write, and was without knowledge of the aforementioned subjects prior to being commissioned as a Prophet. The Prophet was wise to the fullest extent of his mental capacity. God, the Exalted, informed him of some of what had taken place (in the past) and of that which would take place in the future. This is a sign that the Dominion be-

(1) A great scholar of Islam who wrote many works, including one on the Biography of the Prophet .

3

longs to God, and that He is capable over all things."⁽¹⁾

2 Performing Acts for the Sake of God:

The Prophet would always do deeds through which he would seek the pleasure of God. He was harmed and abused when he invited and called people to Islam, yet he was patient and endured all of this, hoping for the reward of God. Abdullah b. Masood said: "The Prophet resembled a prophet who was harmed by his people. He wiped the blood from his face and said, 'O God! Forgive my people, for they know not!'" *(Bukhari)*

Jundub b. Sufyaan said that the Messenger's finger bled during one of the battles, and he said:

"You are but a finger which has bled, which suffers in the path of God." *(Bukhari)*

(1) Qadhi Eiyadh, *Al-Shifa bita'reefi Hoquooqil-Mostafa.*

MUHAMMAD The Messenger of Allah

Sincerity: 3

The Prophet was sincere and honest in all his matters, as God had ordered him. Allah, the Exalted, says:
"Say, 'Indeed, my prayer, my rites of sacrifice, my living and my dying are for God, Lord of the worlds. No partner has He. And this I have been commanded, and I am the first [among you] of the Muslims.'" *[6:162-163]*

Good Morals, Ethics and Companionship: 4

The Prophet was a living example for all humans to follow. His wife A'ishah was asked about his manners, and she said:

"His manners were the Qur'an." *(Muslim)*

In this statement, A'ishah meant that the Prophet abided by its laws and commands

• Muhammad

3

and abstained from its prohibitions, and observed the virtuous deeds mentioned in it. The Prophet ﷺ said:

"God has sent me to perfect good manners and to do good deeds."
(Bukhari & Ahmed)

Allah, the Exalted, described the Prophet ﷺ saying:

"And indeed, you are of a great moral character." *[68:4]*

Anas b. Malik served the Prophet ﷺ for ten years. He was with him day in and day out, both when the Prophet ﷺ traveled and when he was a resident in Madinah. He was thus very knowledgeable of the Prophet's manners. He said:

"The Prophet ﷺ did not swear at anyone, nor was he rude, nor did he curse anyone. If he desired to reprimand someone, he would say, 'What is wrong with him, may dust be cast in his face.'" *(Bukhari)*

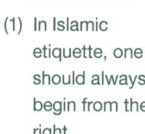

(1) In Islamic etiquette, one should always begin from the right.

Politeness and Good Manners:

The Prophet showed good manners and was courteous to all, even to children. Once when the Prophet was in a gathering, a drink was brought to the Prophet and he drank from it. On his right side there was a young boy and on his left side were elderly men. Feeling obliged by the respect due to elders, and not wanting to hurt the feelings of the child, he asked the young boy:

"Do you mind if I give the drink to them first?' The young boy said, 'O Prophet of God! By God! I would not prefer anyone to drink from the place you drank. This is my fair share[1].' The Messenger of God handed the boy the drink." *(Bukhari)*

"**His manners** were the Qur'an." This means that the Prophet abided by its laws and commands and abstained from its prohibitions.

Love for Reformation and Reconciliation:

Whenever a situation occurred which called for reconciliation, the Prophet would hurry to resolve it. Once when he heard that the people of

• Muhammad

3

Qubaa'[1] disputed with each other about a matter, the Prophet  said: "Let us go to resolve the situation and make peace between them." *(Bukhari)*

7 Ordering with the good and forbidding evil:

If the Prophet saw an act which opposed a tenet of the religion, he would reprimand it in a suitable manner. Abdullah b. Abbas said: The Messenger of God saw a man wearing a gold ring[2], so he reached for it, [and] removed it…. He then said:

"Would one of you seek a burning charcoal and place it on his hand?"

The man was later told, after the Prophet left, "Take your ring! Make good use of it [by selling it]." The man said, "No, by God! I will never take it after the Messenger of God cast it away." *(Muslim)*

Abu Saeed Al-Khudri said:

"I heard the Messenger of Allah say, 'Whoever of you sees an evil must

---

(1) A town previously on the outskirts of Madinah.
(2) It is prohibited for men to wear gold in Islam.

MUHAMMAD The Messenger of Allah

change it with his hand. If he is not able to do so, then he must try to change it by speaking out against it. And if he is not able to do so, then he must hate it his heart. And that is the weakest level of faith.'" *(Muslim)*

Love of Purification: 8

A companion passed by the Prophet ﷺ while he was not in a state of purification. He greeted him with God's name, but the Prophet ﷺ did not return the greeting until he performed ablution and apologized saying:

"I disliked that I should mention God's name while I am not in a state of purity." *(Sahih an-Nasaa'ee, Ibn Khuzaimah)*

إنا فتحنا لك
فتحاً مبيناً

"Indeed, We have given you, [O Muhammad], a clear conquest." *(48:1)*

3

9 Safeguarding and Minding One's Language:

The Messenger of God ﷺ would busy himself with the remembrance of God; he would not talk in vain. He would lengthen his prayers and shorten the speech, and he would not hesitate to help and take care of the needs of someone in need, the poor or the widowed. *(Ibn Hib'ban)*

10 Excelling in Acts of Worship:

A'ishah said, "When the Messenger of Allah ﷺ prayed, he would stand for so long that his feet became swollen." A'ishah asked him, "O Messenger of Allah, are you doing this when Allah has forgiven your past and future sins?" He replied:

"O A'ishah, should I not then be a grateful servant (of God)?" *(Bukhari)*

The Prophet ﷺ would not talk in vain. He would lengthen his prayers and shorten the speech, and he would not hesitate to help and take care of the needs of someone in need, the poor or the widowed.

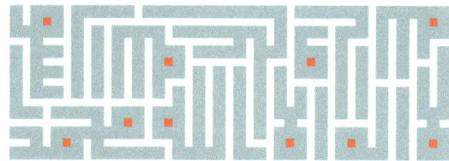

MUHAMMAD The Messenger of Allah

Forbearance: 11

Once some companions came to the Prophet complaining about a tribe, namely the Daws, who refused to accept Islam, asking him to curse them. The Prophet raised his hands in prayer and instead said:
"O Allah guide the tribe of Daws and bring them to Islam!" *(Bukhari and Muslim)*

The Prophet disliked to mention Allah's name while he wasn't in a state of purity.

Good Appearance: 12

The companions knew the Prophet to be the most beautiful of people. One companion said:
"The Prophet was a person of average height. His shoulders were wide. His hair reached his earlobes. Once I saw him adorned in a red garment. I never saw anything more beautiful than him." *(Bukhari)*

3

13   Asceticism in Worldly Affairs:

There are many examples in the Prophet's life which prove that he had no concern for the pleasures of this life. Abdullah b. Masood said:

"The Messenger of God  went to sleep on a mat. He stood up and he had marks on his side due to the mat that he had slept on. We said, 'O Messenger of God, shall we not make [a proper] bedding for you?' He replied, 'What do I have to do with this world? I am only like a traveler that stopped to take shade and rest under a tree, and then leaves it behind and continues on the journey.'" *(Tirmidthi)*

The Prophet was a person of average height. His shoulders were wide. His hair reached his earlobes.

14   Altruism:

Sahl b. Sa'd said, "The Prophet had more care for those around him than for his own self."

"A woman gave the Messenger of God a Burdah (shawl). The Prophet asked his Companions, 'Do you know what a Burdah is?' They replied, 'Yes, O Prophet of God! It is a piece of woven cloth [similar to a shawl].' The woman said, 'O Prophet of God! I have woven this shawl with my own hands for you to wear.' The Messenger of God took it while he direly needed it. After a while, the Messenger of God came out of his home wearing it, and a Companion said to the Messenger of God, 'O Prophet of God! Grant me this shawl to wear!' The Messenger of God said, 'Yes.' He then sat for awhile, then headed back home, folded it and gave it to the person who asked for it. The Companions scolded him saying, 'It was not appropriate for you to ask for his shawl, especially since you know he does not turn anyone down or send them away empty handed!'

The Messenger of Allah did not leave a Dirham or Dinar, or slave, male or female, after his death. He declared a piece of land as an endowment.

3

The man said, 'By God! I only asked him to give it to me because I want to be shrouded in this shawl when I die.' Sahl, the narrator of the Hadeeth, said, 'The shawl was used as a shroud for that man when he died.'" *(Bukhari)*

15 Strong Faith and Dependence on God:

A woman gave the Messenger of Allah a Burdah (shawl) and, though he needed it, he gave it to a person who asked for it.

Although the Prophet and his companions faced severe trials from the disbelievers, he always reminded them that the end was for the believers, and that the Will of God will come to pass. When Abu Bakr and the Prophet hid in a cave after they had left their homes in order to migrate to Madinah, the disbelievers of Makkah had sent scouts in search of them. They came so close to the cave that Abu Bakr could see their feet. Abu Bakr said:

"I looked at the feet of the pagans while we were in the cave

[of Thawr]. I said, 'O Prophet of God! If anyone of them looks down at his feet he would see us!' The Messenger of God said, 'O Abu Bakr! What do you think of two with whom God, the Exalted, is their Third?'" *(Muslim)*

Kindness and Compassion: 16

The Prophet was the kindest of people, and this was also apparent in his treatment of infants.

"The Messenger of God performed Salah (prayer) while he was carrying an infant girl named Umaamah... When he bowed, he put her on the ground, and when he stood up, he would carry her again." *(Bukhari)*

Simplification and Ease: 17

The Prophet always sought to make things easy for people. The Messenger of God said:

"I start the prayer with the intention of lengthening it, but when I hear a child crying, I shorten the prayer, as I know

The Messenger of Allah performed Salah (prayer) while he was carrying a young girl named Umaamah, daughter of Abul-Aas.

its mother would suffer from his distress." *(Bukhari)*

18 Fearing God, being Mindful to not trespass His Limits:

The Messenger of God ﷺ said: "Sometimes, when I return to my family, I would find a date-fruit on the bed. I would pick it up to eat it, but I would fear that it was from the charity[(1)], and thus, put it back." *(Bukhari)*

19 Spending Generously:

Anas b. Malik said:
"The Messenger of God ﷺ was never asked for something when a person accepted Islam, except that he granted that person what he asked. A man came to the Prophet ﷺ and he gave him a herd of sheep that was grazing between two mountains. The man returned to his people and said, 'O my people accept Islam! Muhammad ﷺ gives out generously like one who does not fear poverty.'" *(Muslim)*

The Prophet ﷺ was an example and paradigm to which his people related to in all branches of knowledge; acts of worship, medicine, laws of inheritance, lineage, and other matters as well.

Ibn Abbas said:

"The Prophet was the most generous of people. He was most generous during Ramadan when he met Gabriel . He would meet him every night during Ramadan to practice and review the Qur'an with him. The Messenger of God was so generous, that he was faster than the swiftest wind in this regard." *(Bukhari)*

Abu Dharr said:

"I was walking with the Prophet in the Har'rah (volcanic region) of Madinah and we faced the mount of Uhud. The Prophet said, 'O Abu Dharr!' I replied, 'Here I am O Messenger of God!' He said, 'It would not please me to have an amount of gold equal to the weight of Mount Uhud, until I spend and give it out (in the

(1) It was forbidden by God for the Prophet 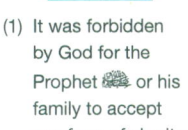 or his family to accept any form of charity.

sake of God) within a night or within three nights. I would keep a single silver piece of it to pay off my debts.'" *(Bukhari)*

Jabir b. Abdullah said:
"The Prophet  did not refuse to give anything which he owned to someone, if they asked for it." *(Bukhari)*

20 Cooperation:

The Prophet was not a king who commanded his followers to carry out his orders. Rather he always carried out his own affairs and helped others in collective duties. A'ishah was once asked about how the Prophet behaved with his family. She said:

A'ishah: "He helped and assisted his family members with their chores, but when the call to prayer was heard, he would leave to attend the prayers."

"He helped and assisted his family members with their chores, but when the call to prayer was heard, he would [stop everything and] leave to attend the prayers." *(Bukhari)*

Al-Baraa bin 'Azib said:
"I saw the Messenger of God

MUHAMMAD The Messenger of Allah

on the Day of the Trench carrying dirt [that was dug from the trench] until his chest was covered with dirt." *(Bukhari)*

Truthfulness: 21

A'ishah said:

"The trait and characteristic which the Prophet hated most was lying. A man would tell a lie in the presence of the Prophet and he would hold it against him, until he knew that he had repented." *(Tirmidthi)*

Even his enemies attested to his truthfulness. Abu Jahl, who was one of the harshest enemies of Islam, said, "O Muhammad! I do not say that you are a liar! I only deny what you brought and what you call people to do." God, the Exalted, says:

"We know that you, [O Muhammad], are saddened by what they say. And indeed, they do not call you untruthful, but it is the verses of Allah that the wrongdoers reject." *[6:33]*

A'ishah, with whom Allah is pleased, said, "The trait and characteristic which the Prophet  hated most was lying."

3

Abdullah bin Al-Harith said, "I have never seen a man who smiled as much as the Messenger of God ﷺ."

22 Sanctifying the limits set by Allah, and Always Seeking the Moderate Path:

A'ishah said:

"The Prophet ﷺ was not given a choice between two matters, except that he chose the easier of the two, as long as it was not a sinful act. If that act was a sinful act, he would be the farthest from it. By God! He never avenged himself. He only became angry when people transgressed the limits and boundaries of God. In that case, he avenged [for the sake of God alone]." *(Bukhari)*

23 Pleasant Facial Expression:

Abdullah bin Al-Harith said:

"I have never seen a man who smiled as much as the Messenger of God ﷺ." *(Tirmidthi)*

24 Honesty, Trustworthiness and Reliability:

The Prophet ﷺ was well-known for his honesty. The pagans of Makkah - who were openly hostile towards him - would leave their valuables with him. His honesty and reliability was tested when the pagans of Makkah abused him and tortured his companions and drove them out of their homes. He ordered his cousin, Ali b. Abi Talib to postpone his migration for three days to return to people their valuables.[1]

Another example of his honesty, trustworthiness and reliability is demonstrated in the Truce of Hudaibiyah. In that famous truce, he agreed to the article in the treaty which stated that any man who left the Prophet would not be returned to him, and any man who left Makkah to join the Prophet would be returned to the pagans. Before the treaty was concluded a man named Abu Jandal b. Amr had managed to escape from the pagans of Makkah and rushed to join Muhammad. The pagans asked Muhammad to honor his pledge and return the escapee. The Messenger of God said:

(1) Ibn Hisham's Biography Vol. 1, p.493 [Arabic Edition].

3

"O Abu Jandal! Be patient and ask God to grant you patience. God will surely help you and those who are persecuted and make it easy for you. We have signed an agreement with them, and we certainly do not betray or act treacherously." *(Baihaquee)*

25. Bravery and courage:

In the Battle of Uhud, the Messenger of Allah ﷺ consulted his Companions. They advised him to fight, while he himself did not see the need to fight.

Ali said:

"You should have seen him on the Day of Badr! We sought refuge with the Messenger of God ﷺ. He was the closest among us to the enemy. On that Day, the Messenger of God ﷺ was the strongest one among us."
(Ahmed)

'Amr b. Al-Haarith said the Messenger of God ﷺ did not leave any gold or silver currency, or a slave, male or female, after his death. He only left behind his white mule, his weapons and a piece of land which he declared as an endowment. *(Bukhari)*

MUHAMMAD The Messenger of Allah

As for his courage and bravery under normal circumstances - Anas b. Malik said:

"The Messenger of God was the best of people and the most courageous. One night, the people of Madinah were frightened and headed towards the sounds they heard during the night. The Messenger of God met them while coming back from the place of the sound, after he made sure that there was no trouble. He was riding a horse that belonged to Abu Talhah without any saddle, and he had his sword with him. He was assuring the people, saying, 'Do not be frightened! Do not be frightened.'" *(Bukhari)*

Unlike other leaders, he did not wait for others to investigate the source of trouble, but he did it himself.

> **The Prophet** was the most generous of people. He was most generous during Ramadan when he met Jibreel.

3

26 Bashfulness and Modesty:

Abu Ayoub Al-Ansari said that the Messenger of Allah ﷺ said:
"Four (traits) are from the practice of the Messengers: modesty, using perfume, using siwak (tooth stick) and marriage." *(Bukhari)*

A'ishah reports that a woman asked the Prophet ﷺ about the bath which is taken at the end of the menstrual period. The Prophet ﷺ said, "Purify yourself with a piece of cloth scented with musk." She sought details, but the Prophet ﷺ felt shy and turned his face. A'ishah said, "I pulled her to myself and told her what the Prophet ﷺ meant." *(Bukhari)*

> **The Prophet ﷺ** was more modest and bashful than a virgin who hides in the women's quarter of the tent.

27 Humility:

The Messenger of God ﷺ was the humblest of people. He was so humble that if a stranger were to enter the mosque and approach the Prophet's sitting place, where he would sit with his

MUHAMMAD The Messenger of Allah

Companions, one would not be able to distinguish him from his Companions.

Anas bin Malik said:

"Once, while we were sitting with the Messenger of God in the Masjid, a man on his camel approached. After he tied it with a rope, he asked, 'Who amongst you is Muhammad?' The Messenger of God was sitting on the ground and leaning on his arm, among his Companions. We directed the Bedouin, saying, 'This white man leaning on his arm.' The Prophet did not differ nor distinguish himself from his Companions." *(Bukhari)*

The Prophet would not hesitate to help the poor, needy and widows. Anas b. Malik said:

"A woman from the people of Madinah, who was partially insane, said to the Prophet, 'I have to ask you [your help] about something.' He helped her and took care of her needs." *(Bukhari)*

The Prophet said, "We certainly do not betray or act treacherously."

3

The Prophet would not hesitate to help the poor, needy and widows.

28 Mercy and Compassion:

Abu Masood Al-Ansari said:
"A man came to the Prophet ﷺ and said, 'O Messenger of God! By God! I do not pray Fajr prayer in congregation because so and so lengthens the prayer.' He said, 'I have never seen the Messenger of God ﷺ deliver a speech in such an angry state.' He said:
'O People! Truly there are among you those who drive people away from good! If you lead people in prayer, shorten the prayer. There are old and weak people and those with special needs behind you in prayer.'" *(Bukhari)*

Once when the Prophet ﷺ went to visit his dying grandchild, he shed tears.

The Messenger of God ﷺ sat holding the child while he was dying. The child's eyes froze in

their places like stones. Upon seeing that, the Messenger of God wept. Sa'd (referring to the tears) said to him, "What is this O' Prophet of God?" He said, "This is a mercy that God, the Exalted, places in the hearts of His slaves. Truly, God is merciful to those who are merciful towards others."
(Bukhari)

Patience and Forbearance: 29

Anas bin Malik said:

"Once, I was walking with the Messenger of God  while he was wearing a Yemeni cloak with a collar with rough edges. A Bedouin grabbed him strongly. I looked at the side of his neck and saw that the edge of the cloak had left a mark on his neck. The Bedouin said, 'O Muhammad! Give me [some] of the wealth of God that you have.' The Messenger of God turned to the Bedouin, laughed and ordered that he be given some money." *(Bukhari)*

The Prophet: "If you lead people in prayer, shorten the prayer. There are old and weak people and those with special needs behind you in prayer."

3

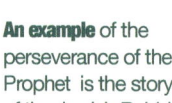

An example of the perseverance of the Prophet is the story of the Jewish Rabbi.

Another example of his patience is the story of the Jewish Rabbi, Zaid bin Sa'nah. Zaid had given something as a loan to the Messenger of God ﷺ. He himself said:

"Two or three days prior to the return of the debt, the Messenger of God ﷺ was attending the funeral of a man from the Ansar. Abu Bakr, Umar, Othman and some other Companions were with the Prophet ﷺ. After he prayed the funeral prayer, he sat down close to a wall, and I came towards him, grabbed him by the edges of his cloak, and looked at him in a harsh way, and said, 'O Muhammad! Will you not pay me back my loan? I have not known the family of Abdul-Mutalib to delay in repaying debts!'

I looked at Umar - his eyes were swollen with anger! He looked at me and said, 'O Enemy of God, do you talk to the Messenger of God and behave towards him in this manner? By the One who sent him with the truth, had it not been for the fear of not entering the Heavenly Gardens, I would have killed you with my sword!' The Prophet ﷺ was looking at Umar in a calm and peaceful manner, and he said, 'O Umar, you should have given us sincere counseling, rather than to do what you did! O Umar, go and repay him his loan, and give him twenty Sa'a (measurement of weight) extra because you scared him!'

Zaid said, 'Umar went with me, and repaid me the debt, and gave me over it twenty Sa'a of dates.' I asked him, 'What is this?' He said, 'The Messenger of God ﷺ ordered me to give it, because I frightened you.' Zaid then asked Umar, 'O Umar, do you know who I am?' Umar said, 'No, I don't - who are you?' Zaid said, 'I am Zaid b. Sa'nah.' Umar inquired, 'The Rabbi?' Zaid answered, 'Yes, the Rabbi.'

Umar then asked him, 'What made you say what you said to the Prophet ﷺ and do what you did to him?' Zaid

The Prophet ﷺ repaid Zaid's loan and gave him over it twenty Sa'a of dates because Umar scared him.

A great example of the Prophet's forgiveness and perseverance is apparent when he pardoned the people of Makkah after its conquest.

3

Zaid said to Umar: "I hold you as a witness that I testify and am satisfied that there is no true god worthy of being worshipped except Allah alone, and Muhammad ﷺ is my Prophet."

answered, 'O Umar, I have seen all the signs of prophethood in the face of the Messenger of God ﷺ except two – (the first) his patience and perseverance precede his anger and the second, the harsher you are towards him, the kinder and more patient he becomes, and I am now satisfied. O Umar, I hold you as a witness that I testify and am satisfied that there is no true god worthy of being worshipped except God alone, and my religion is Islam and Muhammad ﷺ is my Prophet. I also hold you as a witness that half of my wealth - and I am among the wealthiest people in Madinah - I give for the sake of God to the Muslims.'

Umar said, 'You will not be able to distribute your wealth to all the Muslims, so say, 'I will distribute it to some of the followers of Muhammad ﷺ.' Zaid said, 'Then, I will distribute (the apportioned) wealth to some of the Muslims.' Both Zaid and Umar returned to the Messenger of God . Zaid said to him, 'I bear witness that there is no true god worthy of being worshipped except God alone, and that Muhammad  is the slave of God and His Messenger.' He believed in him, and witnessed many battles and then died in the Battle of Tabook while he was encountering the enemy - may God have mercy on Zaid." *(Ibn Hibban)*

Another great example of his forgiveness is apparent when he pardoned the people of Makkah after its conquest. When the Messenger of God gathered the people, who had abused, harmed and tortured him and his companions, and had driven them out of the city of Makkah, he said:

"What do you think I will

do to you?" They answered, "You will only do something favorable. You are a kind and generous brother, and a kind and generous nephew." The Prophet ﷺ said, "Go, for you are free." *(Baihaqi)*

30 Patience:

The Messenger of God ﷺ was the epitome of patience. He was patient with his people before calling them to Islam, for they would worship idols and do sinful acts. He was patient and tolerant with the abuse and harm the pagans of Makkah inflicted on him and

his Companions and sought the reward of God. He was also patient and tolerant with the abuse of the hypocrites in Madinah.

His patience was severely tested when he lost his loved ones. His wife, Khadeejah, died during his lifetime, as did all of his children, except his daughter, Fatimah. His uncles Hamzah and Abu Talib passed away as well. The Prophet was patient and sought the reward of God.

Anas b. Malik said:
"We entered the house of Abu Saif, the blacksmith, with the Prophet ﷺ. Abu Saif's wife was the wetnurse of his son, Ibraheem. The Messenger of God ﷺ lifted his son Ibraheem, smelled him and kissed him. After a while he went and saw his son again - he was dying. The Prophet ﷺ started to cry. Abdurrahmaan b. Auf said, 'O Prophet of God, you too cry?' The Messenger ﷺ said, 'O Ibn Auf, this is a mercy.' The Prophet ﷺ shed more tears and

He was a paradigm of patience when he lost his loved ones. His wife, Khadeejah, died during his lifetime, as did all of his children, except his daughter, Fatimah.

3

The Prophet ﷺ: "The eyes shed tears, the heart is saddened, yet we only say what pleases our Lord. We are saddened by your death, O Ibraheem."

said, 'The eyes shed tears, the heart is saddened, yet we only say what pleases our Lord. We are saddened by your death, O Ibraheem!'" *(Bukhari)*

Justice and Fairness:

31 The Messenger of God ﷺ was just and fair in every aspect of his life and in the application of the religion.

A'ishah said:

"The people of Quraish were extremely concerned about a woman, from a respected tribe called Makhzoom, who committed a theft. They conversed among themselves and said, 'Who can intercede on her behalf with

the Messenger of God so that he can cancel her punishment?'

They finally said, 'Who dares to speak to the Messenger of God in this matter except Usamah b. Zaid, the most beloved young man to the Messenger of God.' So Usamah spoke to the Messenger of God regarding the woman. The Messenger of God said,

'O Usamah! Do you intercede on their behalf to disregard one of God's commanded punishments?'

The Messenger of God got up and delivered a speech, saying:

'People before you were destroyed because when the noble among them stole, they would let them go, and if the poor and weak stole they would punish him.

The people of Quraish were extremely concerned about the Makhzoomi woman who committed a theft.

3

By God! If Fatimah[(1)], the daughter of Muhammad stole, I would carry out her punishment myself." *(Bukhari)*

The Messenger of God was just and fair and allowed others to avenge themselves if he harmed them. Usaid b. Hudhair said:

"A man from the Ansar was cracking jokes with people and making them laugh, and the Prophet passed by him and poked his side lightly with a branch of a tree that he was carrying. The man exclaimed, 'O Prophet of God! Allow me to avenge myself!' The Prophet said, 'Go Ahead!' The man said, 'O Messenger of God, you are wearing a garment, and I was not

A Bedouin grabbed the Prophet strongly and said, "O Muhammad! Give me [some] of the wealth of Allah that you have." He turned to the Bedouin, laughed and ordered that he be given some money.

when you poked me [i.e. you jabbed my exposed skin, so it is only fair I do the same to you]!' The Messenger of God raised his upper garment [to expose his side], and the Ansari [merely] kissed it, saying, 'I only meant to do this, O Messenger of God.'" *(Abu Dawood)*

Fearing God, and Being Mindful of Him: 32

The Messenger of God was the most mindful person of God.

Abdullah bin Masoud said:
"[Once] the Messenger of God said to me, 'Recite to me from the Qur'an.' Abdullah b. Masood said, 'Shall I recite it to you, while it was you to whom it was revealed?' The Prophet said, 'Yes.' He said, 'I started to recite Surat An-Nisaa[(2)], until I reached the ayah:

'So how [will it be] when We bring from every nation a witness and we bring you, [O Muhammad] against these [people] as a witness?' *(4:41)*

(1) Fatimah was the most beloved daughter of the Prophet.
(2) The fourth chapter of the Qur'an.

3

Upon hearing this ayah, the Messenger of God  said, 'That is enough.' Abdullah b. Masood said, 'I turned around and saw the Messenger of God crying.'" *(Bukhari)*

A'ishah said:

"If the Messenger of God saw dark clouds in the sky, he would pace forwards and backwards and would exit and enter his house repeatedly. As soon as it rained, the Prophet would relax. A'ishah asked him about it, and he said, 'I do not know, it may be as some people said:

'And when they saw it as a cloud approaching their valleys, they said, 'This

The Messenger of Allah was just and fair and allowed others to avenge themselves if he harmed them.

is a cloud bringing us rain!' Rather, it is that for which you were impatient; a wind, within it a painful punishment.'"

(Bukhari)

Richness and Contentment of the Heart: 33

Umar b. Al-Khattab said:

"I entered the Messenger's house and I found him sitting on a mat. He had a leather pillow stuffed with fibers. He had a pot of water by his feet, and there were some clothes hung on the wall. His side had marks due to the mat that he lay on. Umar wept when he saw this, and the Messenger asked him, 'Why do you weep?' Umar said, 'O Prophet of God! Khosrau and Caesar enjoy the best of this world, and you are suffering in poverty!' He said, 'Aren't you pleased that they enjoy this world, and that we will enjoy the Hereafter?'" *(Bukhari)*

3

34 Hoping for Good, Even for his Enemies:

A'ishah said:

"I asked the Messenger of God ﷺ, 'Did you face a day harder and more intense than the Battle of Uhud?' He replied, 'I suffered a lot from your people! The worst I suffered was on the Day of Al-'Aqabah when I spoke to [their chief] (in order to support me), but he disappointed me and left me to be harmed by his people. I left the area while I was quite worried, and walked away. When I reached an area called Qarn Ath-Tha'alib, I raised my head to the sky and noticed a cloud that shaded me. Gabriel ﷺ called out to me and said, 'O Muhammad! God, the Exalted, has heard what your people have said to you, and has sent the Angel in charge of the mountains, so that you can command him to do what you please.' The Prophet ﷺ said, 'The Angel in charge of the mountains called me saying, 'May God praise you and keep safe from all evil! O Muhammad,

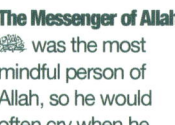

The Messenger of Allah ﷺ was the most mindful person of Allah, so he would often cry when he heard the Qur'an.

MUHAMMAD The Messenger of Allah

I will do whatever you command me to do. If you like I can bring the Akh-shabain mountains together and crush them all.' The Messenger of God said, 'No, it may be that God raises from among them a progeny who worship God alone and associate no partners with Him.'" *(Bukhari)*

It is time to know Him
Rasoulallah.net

This booklet is the third in a series of publications based on a book titled **Muhammad, the Messenger of Allah**. Each booklet covers an aspect of the Prophet's life, deeds and teachings, and aims to provide a better understanding of Islam.

His Lineage, Childhood and Prophethood
Persecution and Hijra
His Manners & Characteristics
The Prophet's Manners With Those Around Him
Textual, Scriptural and Intellectual Testimonials of his Prophethood
Intellectual Proofs of his Prophethood
The Relevance of his Prophethood

www.ingramcontent.com/pod-product-compliance
Lightning Source LLC
LaVergne TN
LVHW070436080526
838202LV00034B/2650